## Kentucky Ecoregions

- ■ Mississippi Alluvial Plain
- ■ Mississippi Valley Loess Plains
- □ Western Allegheny Plateau
- □ Interior River Valleys and Hills
- □ Interior Plateau
- ■ Southwestern Appalachians
- □ Central Appalachians

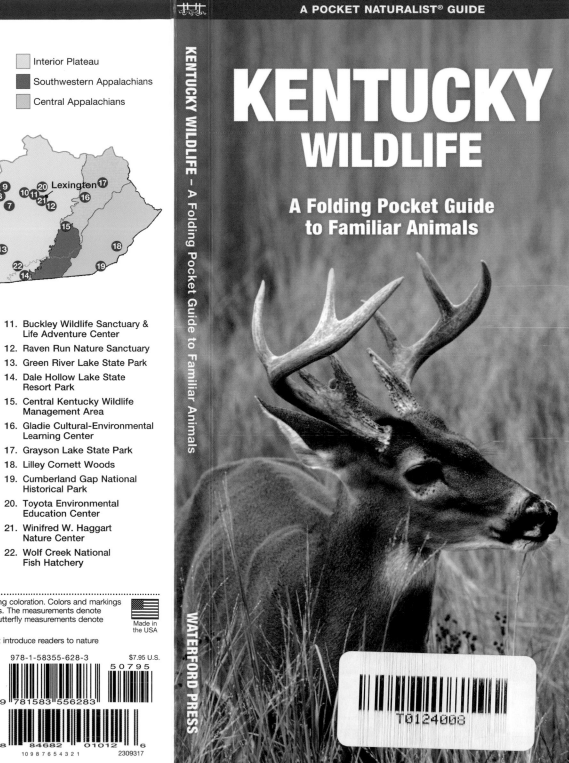

Louisville • Lexington

1. Ballard Wildlife Management Area
2. Clarks River National Wildlife Refuge (NWR)
3. Land Between the Lakes National Recreation Area
4. John James Audubon State Park
5. Otter Creek Outdoor Recreation Area
6. Mammoth Cave National Park
7. Bernheim Arboretum & Research Forest
8. Louisville Nature Center
9. Creasey Mahan Nature Preserve
10. Salato Wildlife Education Center
11. Buckley Wildlife Sanctuary & Life Adventure Center
12. Raven Run Nature Sanctuary
13. Green River Lake State Park
14. Dale Hollow Lake State Resort Park
15. Central Kentucky Wildlife Management Area
16. Gladie Cultural-Environmental Learning Center
17. Grayson Lake State Park
18. Lilley Cornett Woods
19. Cumberland Gap National Historical Park
20. Toyota Environmental Education Center
21. Winifred W. Haggart Nature Center
22. Wolf Creek National Fish Hatchery

Waterford Press publishes reference guides that introduce readers to nature observation, outdoor recreation and survival skills. Product information is featured on the website: www.waterfordpress.com

Text & illustrations © 2011, 2023 Waterford Press Inc. All rights reserved. Photos © Shutterstock. Ecoregion map © The National Atlas of the United States. To order or for information on custom published products, please call 800-434-2555 or email orderdesk@waterfordpress.com. For permissions or to share comments, email editor@waterfordpress.com.

978-1-58355-628-3
$7.95 U.S.

Made in the USA

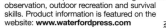

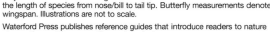

---

# KENTUCKY WILDLIFE

## A Folding Pocket Guide to Familiar Animals

KENTUCKY WILDLIFE – A Folding Pocket Guide to Familiar Animals

WATERFORD PRESS

---

**Black-and-yellow Garden Spider**
*Argiope aurantia*
To 1.25 in. (3.2 cm)

**Fiddleback Spider (Brown Recluse Spider)**
*Loxosceles reclusa*
To .5 in. (1.5 cm)
Easily distinguished by violin-shaped marking on its back. Bites cause tissue degeneration.

**Black Widow Spider**
*Latrodectus mactans*
To .5 in. (1.3 cm)
Venomous spider has a red hourglass marking on its abdomen.

**Roseate Skimmer**
*Orthemis ferruginea*
To 2.25 in. (5.5 cm)
Easily distinguished by its lavender thorax and pinkish abdomen.

**Honey Bee**
*Apis mellifera*
To .75 in. (2 cm)
Slender bee has pollen baskets on its rear legs. Can only sting once. Kentucky's state insect.

**Black Saddlebags**
*Tramea lacerata*
To 2.25 in. (5.2 cm)
Hindwings have large black patches at base. Black abdomen is yellow-spotted.

**Ebony Jewelwing**
*Calopteryx maculata*
To 1.75 in. (4.5 cm)
Like most damselflies, it rests with its wings held together over its back.

**Water Boatman**
Corixidae Family
To .8 cm (.3 in.)
Uses flattened limbs to "row" in quiet, clear waters.

**Green Darner**
*Anax junius*
To 3 in. (8 cm)
Has a bright green thorax and a blue body. Like most dragonflies, it rests with its wings open.

**Deer Tick**
*Ixodes scapularis*
To .25 in. (.6 cm)
Feeds on the blood of mammals and can transmit disease-causing organisms between hosts.

**Water Strider**
*Gerris* spp.
To .5 in. (1.3 cm)
Long-legged insect skates along the surface of the water.

**American Cockroach**
*Periplaneta americana*
To 2 in. (5 cm)

**Firefly**
*Photinus* spp.
To .6 in. (1.5 cm)

**Ladybug Beetle**
Family Coccinellidae
To .5 in. (1.3 cm)

---

**Eastern Tiger Swallowtail**
*Papilio glaucus*
To 6 in. (15 cm)

**Pipevine Swallowtail**
*Battus philenor*
To 3.5 in. (9 cm)
Note white crescent-shaped marks on outer edge of hindwings.

**Black Swallowtail**
*Papilio polyxenes*
To 3.5 in. (9 cm)

**Cloudless Sulphur**
*Phoebis sennae*
To 3 in. (8 cm)
Common in open areas and fields.

**Viceroy**
*Limenitis archippus*
To 3 in. (8 cm)
Told from similar monarch by its smaller size and the thin, black band on its hindwings. Kentucky's state butterfly.

**Buckeye**
*Junonia coenia*
To 2.5 in. (6 cm)

**Monarch**
*Danaus plexippus*
To 4 in. (10 cm)
Note rows of white spots on edges of wings.

**Painted Lady**
*Vanessa cardui*
To 2.5 in. (6 cm)
Tip of forewing is dark with white spots.

**Red Admiral**
*Vanessa atalanta*
To 2.5 in. (6 cm)

**Red-spotted Purple**
*Limenitis arthemis astyanax*
To 3.5 in. (9 cm)

**American Snout**
*Libytheana carinenta*
To 2 in. (5 cm)
"Snout" is formed from projecting mouth parts which enclose its coiled proboscis.

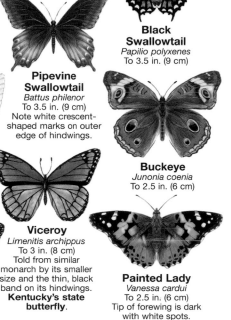

**Luna Moth**
*Actias luna*
To 4.5 in. (11 cm)

**Io Moth**
*Automeris io*
To 3 in. (8 cm)

**Cecropia Silkmoth**
*Hyalophora cecropia*
To 6 in. (15 cm)

**White-lined Sphinx**
*Hyles lineata* To 3.5 in. (9 cm)
Active at all hours, it hovers like a hummingbird.

---

**Rainbow Trout**
*Oncorhynchus mykiss* To 44 in. (1.1 m)
Note reddish side stripe.

**Brown Trout**
*Salmo trutta* To 40 in. (1 m)
Has red and black spots on its body.

**Crappie**
*Pomoxis* spp.
To 16 in. (40 cm)

**Redear Sunfish**
*Lepomis microlophus*
To 14 in. (35 cm)
Also called shellcracker.

**Bluegill**
*Lepomis macrochirus*
To 16 in. (40 cm)

**Smallmouth Bass**
*Micropterus dolomieu* To 27 in. (68 cm)
Jaw joint is beneath the eye.

**Striped Bass**
*Morone saxatilis* To 6 ft. (1.8 m)
Has 6-9 dark side stripes.

**Largemouth Bass**
*Micropterus salmoides* To 40 in. (1 m)
Note prominent side spots. Jaw joint extends past eye.

**White Bass**
*Morone chrysops* To 18 in. (45 cm)
Silvery fish has 4-7 dark side stripes.

**Hybrid Bass**
*Morone* hybrid To 20 in. (50 cm)
Note broken side stripes.

**Kentucky Spotted Bass**
*Micropterus punctulatus* To 2 ft. (60 cm)
Dark spots form lines on sides. Kentucky's state fish.

**Channel Catfish**
*Ictalurus punctatus* To 4 ft. (1.2 m)
Note prominent "whiskers."

**Blue Catfish**
*Ictalurus furcatus* To 5 ft. (1.5 m)
Note straight-edged anal fin. Body lacks dark spots.

**Walleye**
*Sander vitreus* To 40 in. (1 m)
Note white spot on lower lobe of tail.

**Grass Pickerel**
*Esox americanus vermiculatus*
To 16 in. (40 cm)

---

**Yellow-Spotted Salamander**
*Ambystoma maculatum*
To 10 in. (25 cm)

**Bullfrog**
*Lithobates catesbeianus*
To 8 in. (20 cm)
Call is a deep-pitched – jug-o-rum.

**Green Frog**
*Lithobates clamitans*
To 4 in. (10 cm)
Single-note call is a banjo-like twang.

**Gray Treefrog**
*Hyla versicolor*
To 2.5 in. (6 cm)
Call is a strong, resonating trill.

**American Toad**
*Anaxyrus americanus*
To 4.5 in. (11 cm)
Call is a high musical trill lasting up to 30 seconds.

**Ground Skink**
*Scincella lateralis* To 5 in. (13 cm)
Note long tail and dark side stripe.

**Eastern Box Turtle**
*Terrapene carolina*
To 9 in. (23 cm)
Note high-domed shell.

**Timber Rattlesnake**
*Crotalus horridus* To 6 ft. (1.8 m)
Note black tail.

**Mud Snake**
*Farancia abacura* To 7 ft. (2.1 m)
Shiny, dark snake has reddish belly bands extending up its sides.

**Black Rat Snake**
*Elaphe obsoleta obsoleta*
To 8 ft. (2.4 m)

**Northern Ringneck Snake**
*Diadophis punctatus edwardsi*
To 30 in. (75 cm)

**Eastern Hognose Snake**
*Heterodon platirhinos* To 4 ft. (1.2 m)
Thick snake has an upturned snout. Color varies.

**Southern Black Racer**
*Coluber constrictor priapus*
To 6 ft. (1.8 m)
Dark snake has a white chin.

**Eastern Kingsnake**
*Lampropeltis getula getula*
To 7 ft. (2.1 m)
Brown to black snake has a light, chain-like pattern down its back.

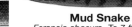

**Copperhead**
*Agkistrodon contortrix* To 52 in. (1.3 m)
Venomous snake has hourglass-shaped bands down its back.

**Milk Snake**
*Lampropeltis triangulum triangulum*
To 7 ft. (2.1 m)

**Canada Goose**
*Branta canadensis*
To 45 in. (1.14 m)

**Wood Duck**
*Aix sponsa* To 20 in. (50 cm)

**Mallard**
*Anas platyrhynchos*
To 28 in. (70 cm)

**American Wigeon**
*Mareca americana* To 23 in. (58 cm)

**Blue-winged Teal**
*Spatula discors* To 16 in. (40 cm)

**Ring-necked Duck**
*Aythya collaris* To 18 in. (45 cm)
Note white ring near bill tip.

**American Coot**
*Fulica americana*
To 16 in. (40 cm)

**Green-winged Teal**
*Anas crecca* To 15 in. (38 cm)

**Killdeer**
*Charadrius vociferus*
To 12 in. (30 cm)
Note two breast bands.

**Great Blue Heron**
*Ardea herodias*
To 4.5 ft. (1.4 m)

**Great Egret**
*Ardea alba*
To 38 in. (95 cm)
Note yellow bill
and black feet.

**Wilson's Snipe**
*Gallinago delicata*
To 12 in. (30 cm)

**Wild Turkey**
*Meleagris gallopavo*
To 4 ft. (1.2 m)

**Ruffed Grouse**
*Bonasa umbellus*
To 19 in. (48 cm)
Note black tail band.

**Northern Bobwhite**
*Colinus virginianus*
To 12 in. (30 cm)

**Eurasian Collared-Dove**
*Streptopelia decaocto*
To 11 in. (28 cm)
Note dark band
on nape.

**White-winged Dove**
*Zenaida asiatica*
To 12 in. (30 cm)
Note prominent
white wing patches.

**Mourning Dove**
*Zenaida macroura*
To 13 in. (33 cm)
Call is a mournful –
ooah-woo-woo-woo.

**Pileated Woodpecker**
*Dryocopus pileatus*
To 17 in. (43 cm)
Note large size.

**Red-bellied Woodpecker**
*Melanerpes carolinus*
To 11 in. (28 cm)

**Downy Woodpecker**
*Dryobates pubescens*
To 6 in. (15 cm)
The similar hairy
woodpecker is
larger and has a
longer bill.

**Northern Flicker**
*Colaptes auratus*
To 13 in. (33 cm)
Wing and tail
linings are
yellow.

**Ruby-throated Hummingbird**
*Archilochus colubris*
To 3.5 in. (9 cm)

**Red-tailed Hawk**
*Buteo jamaicensis*
To 25 in. (63 cm)

**Bald Eagle**
*Haliaeetus leucocephalus*
To 40 in. (1 m)

**Osprey**
*Pandion haliaetus*
To 2 ft. (60 cm)

**Northern Harrier**
*Circus hudsonius*
To 22 in. (55 cm)
Note V-shaped flight
profile and white rump.

**American Kestrel**
*Falco sparverius*
To 12 in. (30 cm)

**Red-eyed Vireo**
*Vireo olivaceus*
To 6 in. (15 cm)

**Great Horned Owl**
*Bubo virginianus*
To 25 in. (63 cm)
Call is a resonant –
hoo-HOO-hoooo.

**Tufted Titmouse**
*Baeolophus bicolor*
To 6 in. (15 cm)

**Carolina Wren**
*Thryothorus ludovicianus*
To 6 in. (15 cm)

**White-breasted Nuthatch**
*Sitta carolinensis*
To 6 in. (15 cm)

**American Crow**
*Corvus brachyrhynchos*
To 22 in. (55 cm)
Call is a distinct – caw.

**Northern Mockingbird**
*Mimus polyglottos*
To 11 in. (28 cm)

**Blue Jay**
*Cyanocitta cristata*
To 14 in. (35 cm)

**Red-winged Blackbird**
*Agelaius phoeniceus*
To 9 in. (23 cm)
Song is a gurgling
– konk-la-reee –
followed by a trill.

**Brown Thrasher**
*Toxostoma rufum*
To 12 in. (30 cm)

**Gray Catbird**
*Dumetella carolinensis*
To 9 in. (23 cm)
Note black cap and
reddish undertail
feathers.

**Wood Thrush**
*Hylocichla mustelina*
To 8 in. (20 cm)
Note rusty head and
spotted breast.

**Eastern Bluebird**
*Sialia sialis*
To 7 in. (18 cm)

**American Robin**
*Turdus migratorius*
To 11 in. (28 cm)

**Eastern Meadowlark**
*Sturnella magna*
To 9 in. (23 cm)

**Prothonotary Warbler**
*Protonotaria citrea*
To 6 in. (15 cm)

**Kentucky Warbler**
*Geothlypis formosus*
To 6 in. (15 cm)
Note dark "sideburns."

**Yellow-breasted Chat**
*Icteria virens*
To 7 in. (18 cm)
Note white
"spectacles."

**Cedar Waxwing**
*Bombycilla cedrorum*
To 7 in. (18 cm)
Red wing marks look
like waxy droplets.

**Yellow-rumped Warbler**
*Setophaga coronata*
To 6 in. (15 cm)
Note yellow on rump
and crown and
white throat.

**Rose-breasted Grosbeak**
*Pheucticus ludovicianus*
To 9 in. (23 cm)

**Scarlet Tanager**
*Piranga olivacea*
To 7 in. (18 cm)

**Northern Cardinal**
*Cardinalis cardinalis*
To 9 in. (23 cm)
Kentucky's state bird.

**American Goldfinch**
*Spinus tristis*
To 5 in. (13 cm)

**House Finch**
*Haemorhous mexicanus*
To 6 in. (15 cm)

**Baltimore Oriole**
*Icterus galbula*
To 8 in. (20 cm)

**Blue Grosbeak**
*Passerina caerulea*
To 8 in. (20 cm)

**Indigo Bunting**
*Passerina cyanea*
To 6 in. (15 cm)

**Virginia Opossum**
*Didelphis virginiana*
To 40 in. (1 m)
Note long fur and naked tail.

**Eastern Gray Squirrel**
*Sciurus carolinensis*
To 20 in. (50 cm)
Kentucky's state
wild game animal.

**Eastern Red Bat**
*Lasiurus borealis*
To 5 in. (13 cm)

**Fox Squirrel**
*Sciurus niger*
To 28 in. (70 cm)
Note large size and
bushy tail. Largest
squirrel in the U.S.

**Long-tailed Weasel**
*Mustela frenata*
To 21 in. (53 cm)
Note brown feet and
yellowish neck.

**Southern Flying Squirrel**
*Glaucomys volans*
To 10 in. (25 cm)

**Deer Mouse**
*Peromyscus maniculatus*
To 8 in. (20 cm)
Has white belly
and a hairy tail.

**Eastern Woodrat**
*Neotoma floridana*
To 18 in. (45 cm)

**Swamp Rabbit**
*Sylvilagus aquaticus*
To 22 in. (55 cm)

**Eastern Cottontail**
*Sylvilagus floridanus*
To 18 in. (45 cm)

**Woodchuck**
*Marmota monax*
To 32 in. (80 cm)

**Common Raccoon**
*Procyon lotor*
To 40 in. (1 m)

**Northern River Otter**
*Lontra canadensis*
To 52 in. (1.3 m)

**Common Muskrat**
*Ondatra zibethicus*
To 2 ft. (60 cm)
Aquatic rodent has
a naked, scaly tail.

**Mink**
*Neovison vison*
To 28 in. (70 cm)
Chin is white.

**Striped Skunk**
*Mephitis mephitis*
To 32 in. (80 cm)

**American Beaver**
*Castor canadensis*
To 4 ft. (1.2 m)

**Red Fox**
*Vulpes vulpes*
To 40 in. (1 m)
Note white-tipped tail.

**Common Gray Fox**
*Urocyon cinereoargenteus*
To 3.5 ft. (1.1 m)
Note black-tipped tail.

**Wild Boar**
*Sus scrofa* To 6 ft. (1.8 m)
Introduced species is
descended from the
Eurasian wild boar.

**Coyote**
*Canis latrans*
To 52 in. (1.3 m)

**Bobcat**
*Lynx rufus*
To 4 ft. (1.2 m)

**Black Bear**
*Ursus americanus*
To 6 ft. (1.8 m)

**White-tailed Deer**
*Odocoileus virginianus* To 7 ft. (2.1 m)
Fluffy tail is white below and held
aloft when running.

**Elk**
*Cervus canadensis*
To 10 ft. (3 m)